Halloween Howlers

FRIGHTFULLY FUNNY KNOCK-KNOCK JOKES

BY MICHAEL TEITELBAUM
PICTURES BY JANNIE HO

HARPER FESTIVAL

An Imprint of HarperCollinsPublishers

Knock, knock!
  Who's there?
Into!
  Into who?
Into days it will
be Halloween!

Knock, knock!
  Who's there?
Witch!
  Witch who?

Knock, knock!
  Who's there?
Howl!
  Howl who?
Howl you be dressing up
this Halloween?

SPOOKTACULAR
SALE

VAMPIRE BLOOD PAINT

MUMMY BANDAGES
100ft $5

$50

Knock, knock!
Who's there?
Mummy!
Mummy who?

Knock, knock!
  Who's there?
Bee!
  Bee who?
Bee-ware!
It's Halloween!

Knock, knock!
  Who's there?
Howdy!
  Howdy who?

Trick
or
Treat

Knock, knock!

Who's there?

Ice cream!

Ice cream who?

Knock, knock!
Who's there?
ock, knock!
Who's there?
rror!
Horror who?
rror you going
carry all that
andy?

Knock, knock!
Who's there?
Common!
Common who?

Knock, knock!
Who's there?
Ghost!
Ghost who?
Ghost stand over there and I'll bring you some punch!

Zombie afraid— it's just a costume!

Knock, knock!
Who's there?
Virgo!
Virgo who?
Virgo-ing to visit a graveyard. Wanna come?

Knock, knock!
Who's there?
Bury!
Bury who?
Bury scary, all these ghosts and monsters!

Here lies
Drak U. Larr
For the
time being

Here lies
Frank N. Stein
At least,
certain
parts of
him

Here li
Frank N. St
Other
Parts of
him

Here lies
Smiley the
Clown...
He died
laughing

Knock, knock!
Who's there?
Goblin!
Goblin who?

Knock, knock!
Who's there?
Ghouls!
Ghouls who?

Here lies
I.M. Terrified
Scared to
death

Knock, knock!
Who's there?
Bat!
Bat who?
Bat you can't guess where we are going next!

Knock, knock!
Who's there!
Displace!
Displace who?
Displace is a wreck!
And creepy, too!

Knock, knock!
Who's there?
Spider!
Spider who?

Knock, knock!
Who's there?
Disguise!
Disguise who?
Disguise giving me
the creeps!

Knock, knock!
Who's there?
Toucan!
Toucan who?

ock, knock!
 Who's there?
mpaign!
 Campaign who?

Knock, knock!
 Who's there?
Wheel!
 Wheel who?
 Wheel go downstairs
 and see what's there!

Knock, knock!
Who's there!
Fangs!
Fangs who?

Knock, knock!
Who's there?
All done!
All done who?

Knock, knock!
Who's there?
Water!
Water who?

Knock, knock
Who's there?
Lettuce!
Lettuce who?
Lettuce get out of here and go home!

Knock, knock!
 Who's there?
Boo!
 Boo who?
Don't cry. Halloween will come
again next year!